HEIFETZ *Collection*

HAVANAISE

for Violin and Piano

CAMILLE SAINT-SAËNS, Op. 83

Critical Urtext Edition

Edited by Endre Granat

KEISER

FOREWORD

The *Havanaise* (*Habanera* in French) by Camille Saint-Saëns op.83 dates from 1885-87. The composer dedicated this work to Rafael Diaz Albertini, a violinist of Cuban origin. In 1888 Saint-Saëns completed the orchestration of the *Havanaise* . This Critical Urtext Edition is based on the composer's manuscript, the first print of the violin and piano version, and to a large part, on the historic recording by the composer himself with the violinist Gabriel Willaume (1919).

Endre Granat

HAVANAISE
for Violin and Piano

CAMILLE SAINT-SAËNS, Op. 83

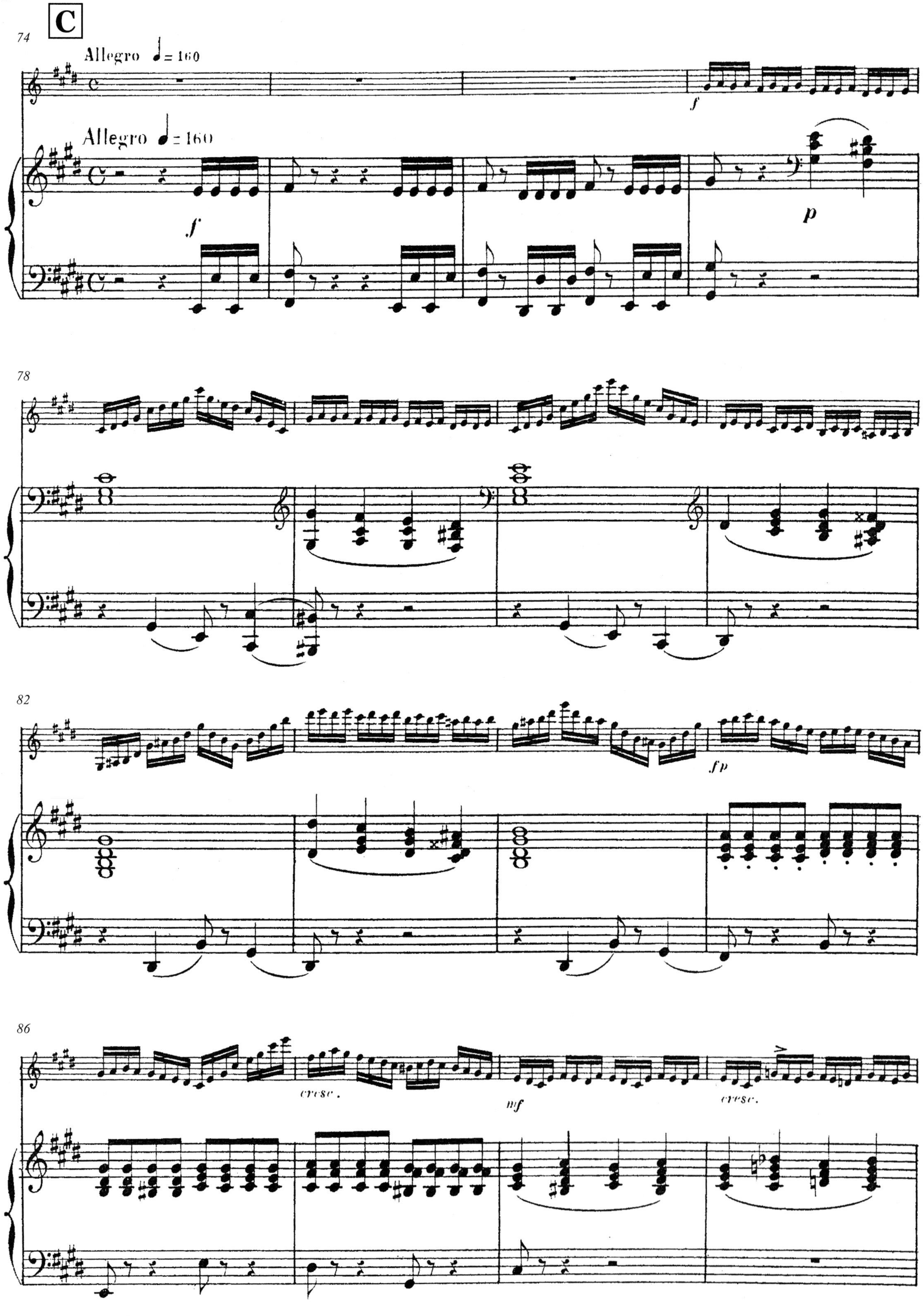
C
74
Allegro ♩= 160
Allegro ♩= 160
f
f
p
78
82
fp
86
cresc.
mf
cresc.

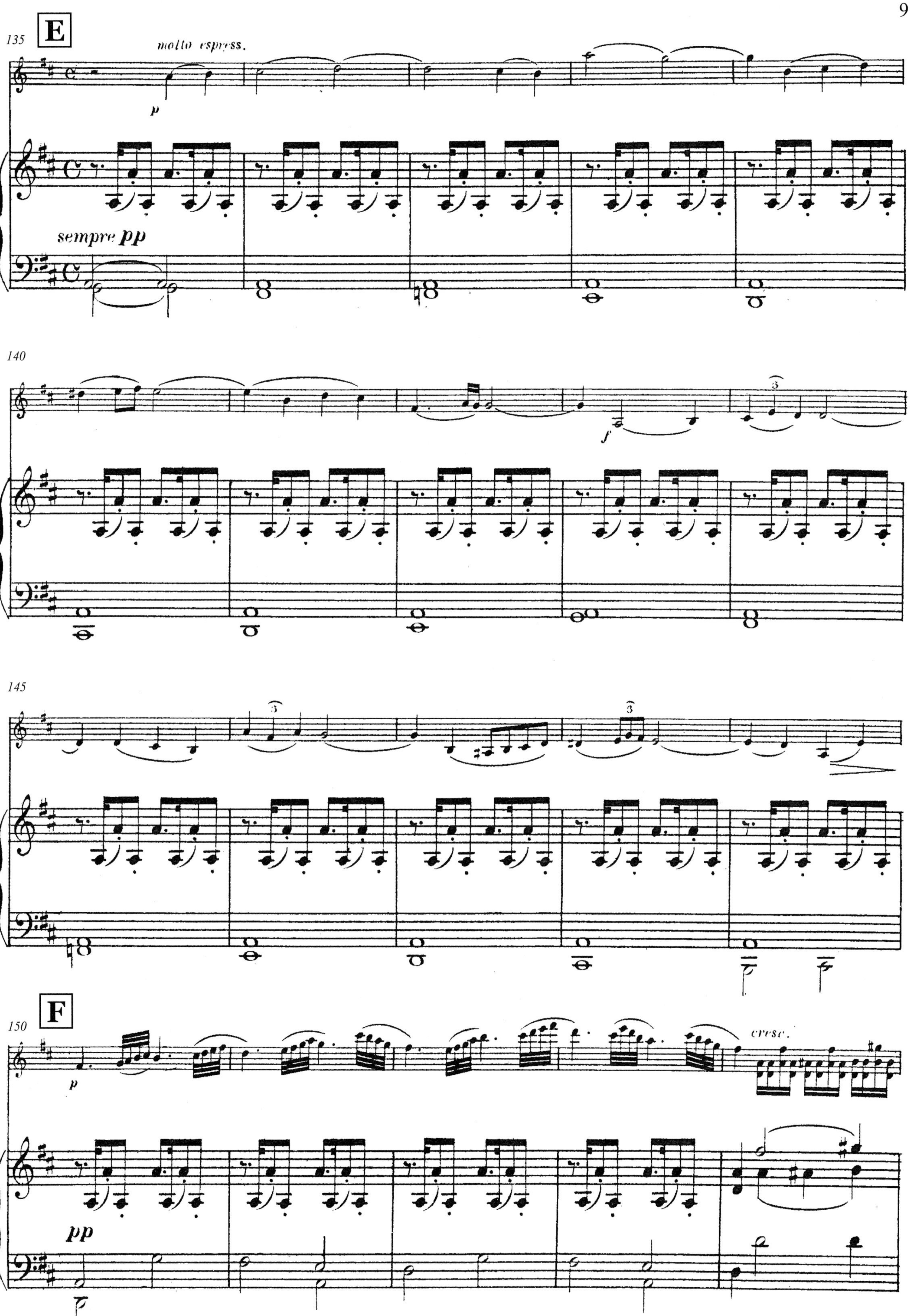
E
molto espress.
sempre pp
F
cresc.

12